AVIATION

B-29 Superfortress, Vol. 1

Boeing's XB-29 through B-29B in World War II

DAVID DOYLE

SCHIFFER MILITARY
4880 Lower Valley Road Atglen, PA 19310

Library of Congress Control Number: 2019947419

Designed by Justin Watkinson
Technical Layout by Jack Chappell
Type set in Impact/Minion Pro/Univers LT Std
Front cover photo courtesy of Rick Kolasa

ISBN: 978-0-7643-5937-8
Printed in China

Published by Schiffer Publishing, Ltd.
4880 Lower Valley Road
Atglen, PA 19310
Phone: (610) 593-1777; Fax: (610) 593-2002
E-mail: Info@schifferbooks.com
www.schifferbooks.com

Acknowledgments

I have been blessed with the generous help of many friends and colleagues when preparing this manuscript. Truly, this book would not have been possible without their collective assistance. Tom Kailbourn, Rich Kolasa, Stan Piet, Scott Taylor, Dana Bell, Bill Larkins, Tracy White, the San Diego Air & Space Museum, the staff at the Air Force Historical Research Agency, and Brett Stolle at the National Museum of the United States Air Force all gave of their time without hesitation. My lovely and dear wife, Denise, scanned photos, proofread manuscripts, and was my personal cheerleader throughout the difficult parts of this project, and without her unflagging support this could not have been completed.

All photos are from the collection of the National Museum of the United States Air Force, unless otherwise noted.

Contents

Introduction

Despite the Japanese attack on Pearl Harbor being the event that drew the United States into World War II, the nation's earliest strategic-bombing efforts were focused on the European theater. One of the reasons for this was the great distances of the Pacific. The B-17s and B-24s, which served so well in Europe, simply did not have the range to strike Japan. This was by no means a surprise to US war strategists.

In October 1937, Army Air Force chief of staff Oscar Westover issued an informal design request for an extremely long-range heavy bomber. In the following years, as the world condition deteriorated, the need for such an aircraft became increasingly apparent. An Air Corps committee, chaired by Brig. Gen. W. G. Kilner, studied the future needs of the Air Corps. Incidentally, among the members of the committee was Charles Lindbergh. The committee's report of June 1939 included the recommendation that long-range heavy bombers be developed. On January 29, 1940, the Air Corps issued Request for Data R-40B and Specification XC-218, which laid out a so-called superbomber capable of delivering 20,000 pounds of bombs to a target 2,667 miles away and capable of flying at a speed of 400 miles per hour (mph). In April, citing lessons learned in Europe, the specifications were revised to include self-sealing fuel tanks and to bolster armor and armament. The specification package was submitted to Boeing, Consolidated, Douglas, and Lockheed. On June 27, 1940, the Air Corps issued each of these four firms contracts for preliminary engineering data related to the new superbomber. The Lockheed submission was designated XB-30, the Douglas the XB-31, the Consolidated the XB-32, and the Boeing the XB-29. Douglas and Lockheed almost immediately withdrew from the competition before completing any detailed design work.

Boeing, anticipating the need for such an aircraft, had begun design work at its own expense as far back as 1938. Thus, when the Air Corps issued the 1940 request, Boeing already had a significant amount of design work done. It is not surprising then that on August 24, 1940, the Army awarded the company a contract for two prototypes and a static test example of the XB-29. A few days later, Consolidated was awarded a contract to produce two XB-32 aircraft as well.

Boeing completed a full-scale mockup of the XB-29 in November, with the result that a third prototype was ordered the next month.

B-29 Specifications

Wingspan	141 ft., 2 in.
Length	99 ft.
Height	27 ft., 9 in.
Empty weight	70,140 lbs.
Loaded weight	135,000 lbs.
Power plant	Four 2,200 hp Wright R-3350-23 Cyclone 18-cylinder air-cooled engines,
	each with a pair of General Electric B-11 superchargers
Armament	Ten 0.5-in. machine guns and one 20 mm cannon
Maximum speed	375 mph
Cruising speed	200–250 mph
Service calling	31,850 ft.
Range	3,250 miles
Crew	11

The Model 294 was Boeing's response for an Army Air Corps requirement in 1934 for a heavy, very long-range (5,000-mile radius) bomber. Successively redesignated the XBLR-1 and the XB-15, this plane was at the time the largest aircraft yet constructed in the United States, having a wingspan of 149 feet and an overall length of 87 feet. Though this plane did not go into series production, it gave Boeing a large advantage when it developed the B-29 a few years later.

Douglas Aircraft was a contender in the program to develop a very heavy bomber, with its XB-19 (originally, XBLR-2). The plane first flew in June 1941, and the Army Air Forces used it for testing until 1946. Once again, this plane failed to be approved for series production.

The Air Forces contracted with Consolidated to produce the B-32 Dominator, of similar size and capabilities to the Boeing B-29. The intention was to have the Dominator as a backup should the nascent Boeing B-29 program fail or hit serious delays. Indeed, 118 production Dominators, designated B-32, were delivered, some of which served in the Pacific in the final days of World War II. This aircraft is seen at Yontan Airstrip, Okinawa, on August 25, 1945. *National Archives*

On April 9, 1945, the final Boeing-built B-17 was rolled out of the Seattle plant, covered in markings indicating each of the targets struck by B-17s to that point. Standing alongside was a B-29, the company's then-new product gaining fame in the Pacific, which was similarly adorned. *Air Force Historical Research Agency*

CHAPTER 1

XB-29

The transition from drawing to formed aluminum presented some challenges. The B-29, which—building on the reputation of its predecessor—was dubbed the Superfortress, was the most advanced aircraft produced during World War II in the United States—arguably, in fact, in the world. It was also the most expensive weapons system of World War II, costing over three billion dollars, 50 percent more than the atomic bomb project.

When the first XB-29, serial number 41-0002, finally took to the air on September 21, 1942, it was over six months behind schedule. While the airframe itself was proving to be a sound design, the newly and hurriedly developed giant Wright R-3350-12 twin-row, eighteen-cylinder engines were proving to be trouble prone. The engines were trouble-prone to overheating and, once hot, susceptible to catching fire. Boeing's chief test pilot Edmund T. "Eddie" Allen was at the controls for the first and many of the subsequent test flights.

The XB-29 had logged only twenty-seven hours in the air out of twenty-three test flights by December. During that time, sixteen engines had been replaced, as had twenty-two carburetors, and there had been nineteen revisions to the exhaust system. During a December 28, 1942, test flight, one of the engines caught fire in air, leading Allen to immediately return to Boeing Field.

The second XB-29, serial number 41-0003, first flew two days later, but it too suffered an engine fire, causing its maiden flight to be cut short as the aircraft returned to Boeing Field. Using engines borrowed from the first XB-29, 41-0003 again took to the air on February 18, 1943. Eight minutes into the flight, an engine fire again broke out. Unable to extinguish the fire, Allen turned the Superfortress toward Boeing Field. Sadly, the fire burned through the main wing spar before Allen could reach the runway. The wing buckled and the burning bomber fell from the sky, landing on the Frye Meat Packing Plant, killing nineteen Frye workers as well as Allen and the rest of the eleven-man XB-29 flight crew. A fireman responding to the fire also perished.

The third and final XB-29, serial number 41-18335, incorporated numerous revisions to the engines in light of the problems with the first two Superfortresses. This aircraft first flew in June 1943 and was subsequently named "Gremlin Hotel."

The first XB-29, serial number 41-0002, spent the war at the Boeing plant as a test bed and was fittingly named the "Flying Guinea Pig." The Flying Guinea Pig survived the war and was scrapped in 1948.

The first XB-29 is parked on a hardstand. A tow bar is attached to the nose landing gear, and a window on the cockpit canopy is open. With the exception of the lack of turrets, the presence of the three-bladed propellers, and some other details, the basic shape of the airframe was the same one that would continue throughout B-29 production.

The XB-29 prototypes lacked a tail turret and any other armaments. Clear blisters for observation were installed on the waist of the fuselage. A bumper on the bottom of the aft fuselage between the horizontal stabilizers protected the tail from damage during excessively nose-high takeoffs or landings. *San Diego Air & Space Museum*

The first of thee flying prototype Boeing XB-29s (a fourth airframe was built as a static-test article) bore tail number 1002, representing its serial number, 41-002. This plane was painted in camouflage of Olive Drab over Neutral Gray and was equipped with three-bladed, 17-foot-diameter Hamilton Standard Hydromatic propellers. The XB-29s had two bomb bays: one forward of the wings and one aft of the wings. *San Diego Air & Space Museum*

Boeing XB-29, serial number 41-002, is viewed from the front, with the tow bar still attached to the nose gear. Each cowling had a large scoop on the chin, for engine-air induction. The nose gear and the main landing gear had twin wheels, one on each side of the oleo struts.

The first XB-29, serial number 41-002, takes off on a test flight. Starting on September 15, 1942, the first prototype began making short "hops" from the runway, and on September 21 it took off on its first flight, with Eddie Allen, from Boeing's Flight Test and Aeronautics Department, in the pilot's seat. The early flights of the XB-29s would be plagued by nearly constant problems and failures of the Wright R-3350-13 engine, which was a new power plant that was rushed into production. Eventually, the problems with the R-3350s would be fixed, and versions of these engines would power all production B-29s. *San Diego Air & Space Museum*

Boeing XB-29, serial number 41-002, flies above a mountainous area. By the time this photo was taken, four turrets (possibly mockups) and a tail turret (definitely a mockup) had been installed on the fuselage.

The first XB-29 began static ground tests of its engines on September 8, 1942. At this point, the tail number had not yet been applied to the dorsal fin. At the top of that fin was a short mast with two pitot tubes projecting from the front of it.

All four Wright R-3350 radial engines are running in this overhead view of the first XB-29 during the first static tests of the engines, on the night of September 8, 1942. Atop the fuselage, round fairings are visible at the two places where it was intended that the top, remote-controlled turrets would be installed.

The third XB-29 prototype, serial number 41-18335, had its first flight in June 1943. Painted in white in small letters below the cockpit canopy was the nickname, "Gremlin Hotel." Note the radio direction-finder (RDF) loop antenna inside the teardrop-shaped aircraft commander's observation blister, just aft of the canopy.

"Gremlin Hotel" flies high above a mountain range during a test flight. On the sides of the nacelles are the visible parts of the turbosuperchargers. The XB-29s and subsequent models of the Superfortress had two superchargers, to cope with the massive amount of air the carburetors required. Each engine had a built-in conventional supercharger, supplemented by an external turbosupercharger. Jutting from the recess in the side of each engine nacelle is the flight hood, through which exhaust gases were expelled.

Like the first two XB-29 prototypes, the third one lacked a tail turret; as a result, the rudder was slightly taller than on production B-29s. One aspect of the third prototype that differed from its two predecessors was the presence of three spherical domes in the waist of the fuselage: one on top and one on each side. These were sighting domes for the gunners who would operate, remotely, the machine gun turrets.

The third XB-29 shows off its sleek, streamlined contours during a test flight. Of note is the dark-colored rudder, which, along with the other control surfaces, was fabric covered. The third prototype had numerous modifications to correct the many deficiencies of the first two prototypes. To assist in getting Boeing's new Wichita, Kansas, plant up to speed, this plane was dispatched there as a reference tool. *National Archives*

CHAPTER 2

YB-29

In May 1941, well before the first flight of a Superfortress, the Army Air Corps ordered fourteen service test examples, designated YB-29. These aircraft would not be built in Boeing's Seattle plant, but rather in a new, purpose-built facility in Wichita, Kansas. The engines were improved Wright R-3350-21 models.

The fuselage of the YB-29, and indeed all the Superfortresses, was innovative in that the crew compartment was pressurized, a first for a bomber. Pressurization did away with the need for the bulky and awkward oxygen gear that had to be worn by B-17 and B-24 crews. Notably, the pressurized crew compartments were heated, also doing away with the extremely bulky, insulated, and electrically heated flying suits worn by crews of the earlier bombers.

At the front of the B-29 fuselage was the forward pressurized compartment, including the bombardier's station; pilot's and copilot's seats; and engineer's, navigator's, and radio operator's stations. This was followed by the unpressurized fore and aft bomb bays. Behind the aft bomb bay was another pressurized compartment and finally the tail section, which included a tiny pressurized position for the tail gunner.

Above the bomb bays was a pressurized tube known as the communication tunnel, which connected the fore and aft pressurized compartments. Turbines driven by the inboard engines provided cabin pressurization air and 70-degree heat. Pressurization was typically employed at altitudes over 8,000 feet. However, in combat zones the crew typically wore oxygen masks in the event enemy gunfire caused a loss of cabin pressurization.

The first of the YB-29s, serial number 41-36954, was completed by Boeing Wichita on April 15, 1943, and flew for the first time on June 26, 1943. By July, seven of the aircraft had been delivered to the Army Air Force and were equipping training units.

The YB-29 aircraft carried serial numbers 41-36954 and 41-36967.

The production of the B-29 would be split between several manufacturers: Boeing at Renton, Washington, and Wichita, Kansas; Martin at Omaha, Nebraska; and Bell at Marietta, Georgia. The YB-29, the service-test model of the Superfortress, of which fourteen were produced, was manufactured at Boeing's Wichita plant. As seen in this photo of the first YB-29, serial number 41-36954, under construction, the service-test planes were equipped with the turrets, including the tail turret.

Boeing YB-29, serial number 41-36960, and another YB-29 with an indistinct tail number were photographed from a third plane, likely another YB-29. Bare aluminum is present on the leading edges of the wings, horizontal stabilizers, and dorsal fin where the deicer boots had been removed. The YB-29's first flight was June 26, 1943. By that time, Gen. Henry H. "Hap" Arnold had approved the B-29 program as a "Special Project," which combined the production, modifications, testing, labor and crew training, and operational organization under a single, high-priority program, to expedite getting the Superfortress into the war as quickly as possible. The YB-29s played an important role in the early stages of the Special Project. *National Archives*

Similar to the heavily armed Boeing YB-40 experimental bomber-escort based on the B-17F, the fourth YB-29, serial number 41-36957, served as a test plane for a proposed bomber-escort, to be armed with additional remote-controlled turrets. As seen in a side photo of the plane, extra turrets were mounted on the nose and on the fuselage sides aft of the cockpit and aft of the wings. Also, a 20 mm cannon was installed in each existing twin .50-caliber machine gun turret.

The nose of the up-gunned YB-29 included an ERCO ball turret in the nose. To achieve this, the nose was modified, eliminating the forward, clear part of the nose and substituting a metal fairing to support the turret.

YB-29, serial number 41-36957, is observed from the left rear following its conversion to an experimental bomber-escort. The two clear domes for sighting on the sides of the waist of the stock YB-29 were replaced by new, twin .50-caliber machine gun turrets.

The ball turret in the nose of the YB-29 bomber-escort and the left forward side turret are seen from a close perspective in a hangar. The forward side turrets were of a type that had been developed for the Convair PB4Y-2 Privateer. The guns traversed along a fore-and-aft slot on the turret housing, with a zippered canvas closure on the slot.

The aft ventral turret is traversed to the left, showing the additional 20 mm cannon that had been added between the two .50-caliber machine guns. Farther forward is the aft side turret, with two .50-caliber machine gun barrels protruding from it.

The tail turret of the YB-29s had a single M2 20 mm cannon between two .50-caliber machine guns, and this arrangement was what was used on the YB-29 bomber-escort prototype.

As seen from the rear, the opening for the guns in the rear turret had a canvas boot to keep out the elements.

CHAPTER 3

B-29

Even before the first XB-29 had flown, 250 B-29 production bombers had been ordered, with those aircraft to be built in a government-owned plant to be constructed near Wichita, Kansas, and operated by Boeing. In February 1942, still before the first flight of a Superfortress, the orders were increased to 500 aircraft. The next month, over 1,000 more were placed on order, those aircraft to be produced not by Boeing, but by Bell, North American, and General Motors. Soon enough, it was decided to remove North American from the pool, replacing that allocation with those assigned to a new Boeing facility in Renton, Washington. The Renton-produced aircraft would be the B-29As, described in the next chapter. Later, even though the government-owned plant built in Cleveland was virtually complete, General Motors was removed from the production pool, its place taken by Martin. GM did produce numerous large subassemblies for the B-29 in its Cleveland plant, which were fed to other B-29 assembly plants.

Boeing completed the first production B-29 in Wichita in September 1943. Ultimately, the Wichita plant produced 1,620 B-29s, while, beginning in February 1944, Bell built 357 in Marietta, Georgia, and from mid-1944 onward, Martin built 536 in Omaha, including the aircraft that were to deliver the atomic bombs.

The defensive armament initially installed consisted of four multiple-gun, remote-controlled gun turrets, two on the top and two on the bottom. When production began, all four turrets featured twin .50-caliber machine guns. But just as with its predecessor, the B-17, the B-29 proved to be vulnerable to frontal attack. Beginning at Boeing-Wichita block 40 and Bell block 10, the forward top turret was changed to a quad .50-caliber unit—the same turret found on the top of many Northrop P-61 Black Widows. This turret was used on all Martin B-29 model aircraft as well. Whether two or four gun, the turrets were not pressurized. The weapons were operated by remote control via the General Electric 2CFR55B1 Central Station Fire Control System. A GE type CH computer was linked to the sight at each gunner's station (top gunner, bombardier, and two waist gunners). Through this system, a single gunner could control multiple gun installations. At the tail of the aircraft was a gunner with a pair of .50-caliber machine guns and, initially, a 20 mm autocannon. The autocannon proved problematic and was not installed after Wichita block 55, Martin block 25, or Bell block 25. It was often removed in the field as well.

As a very heavy bombardment aircraft, although the suite of remote-controlled multiple gun turrets was impressive, the primary armament of the B-29 was bombs. The normal bombload of the Superfortress was forty 500-pound bombs; other load options for conventional B-29s included eighty 100-pound, fifty-six 300-pound, twelve 1,000-pound, twelve 1,600-pound, eight 2,000-pound, or four 4,000-pound bombs.

Boeing-Wichita

Production block	Starting serial number	Ending serial number
B-29-1-BW	42-6205	42-6254
B-29-5-BW	42-6255	42-6304
B-29-10-BW	42-6305	42-6354
B-29-15-BW	42-6355	42-6404
B-29-20-BW	42-6405	42-6454
B-29-25-BW	42-24420	42-24469
B-29-30-BW	42-24470	42-24519
B-29-35-BW	42-24520	42-24569
B-29-40-BW	42-24570	42-24669
B-29-45-BW	42-24670	42-24769
B-29-50-BW	42-24770	42-24869
B-29-55-BW	42-24870	42-24919
	44-69655	44-69704
B-29-60-BW	44-69705	44-69804
B-29-65-BW	44-69805	44-69904
B-29-70-BW	44-69905	44-70004
B-29-75-BW	44-70005	44-70104
B-29-80-BW	44-70105	44-70154
	44-87584	44-87633
B-29-85-BW	44-87634	44-87683
B-29-86-BW	44-87684	44-87733
B-29-90-BW	44-87734	44-87783
B-29-95-BW	45-21758	45-21792
	45-21813	45-21842
B-29-96-BW	45-21793	45-21812
B-29-97-BW	45-21743	45-21757
B-29-100-BW	45-21843	45-21872

Bell-Marietta

Production block	Starting serial number	Ending serial number
B-29-1-BA	42-6222, 42-6224, 42-6233, 42-6235, 42-6243	
	42-63352	42-63365
B-29-5-BA	42-63366	42-63381
B-29-10-BA	42-63382	42-63401
B-29-15-BA	42-63402	42-63451
B-29-20-BA	42-63452	42-63501
B-29-25-BA	42-63502	42-63551
B-29-30-BA	42-63552	42-63580

Martin-Omaha

Production block	Starting serial number	Ending serial number
B-29-1-MO	42-6229, 42-6230, 42-6231, 42-6232, 42-6237	
	42-65202	42-65204
B-29-5-MO	42-65205	42-65211
B-29-10-MO	42-65212	42-65219
B-29-15-MO	42-65220	42-65235
B-29-20-MO	42-65236	42-65263
B-29-25-MO	42-65264	42-65313
B-29-30-MO	42-65315	42-65383
B-29-35-MO	42-65384	42-65401
	44-27259	44-27325
B-29-40-MO	44-27326	44-27358
	44-86242	44-86276
B-29-45-MO	44-86277	44-86315
B-29-50-MO	44-86316	44-86370
B-29-55-MO	44-86371	44-86425
B-29-60-MO	44-86426	44-86473

The Boeing B-29, with no model designation letter following the designation, was the first production model of the Superfortress. This model was produced at three factories: Boeing-Wichita (Kansas), Martin-Omaha (Nebraska), and Bell-Marietta (Georgia). A key feature of the B-29 was the construction of the wing: the inboard sections, which spanned from the outboard sides of the two outboard engine nacelles, were bolted together where they passed through the interior of the fuselage. Outboard wing sections spanned from the outboard nacelles to the wingtips. Shown here in flight over a prairie is Boeing B-29-1-BW, serial number 42-6242. (BW was the suffix for Boeing-Wichita, BA for Bell-Marietta, and MO for Martin-Omaha.)

Boeing B-29-1-BW, serial number 42-6242, is viewed from below during a flight. The B-29s entered production at Boeing-Wichita in September 1943, at Bell-Marietta in February 1944, and at Martin-Omaha in May 1944.

The B-29s were powered by the Wright R-3350-23 engines, rated at 2,200 horsepower. These engines continued to have problems, sometimes catching fire in flight. This was caused by several issues, but in short the engines tended to run too hot, sometimes causing the destruction of the exhaust valves. Wright and the Army continued to work on fixes to these problems. As seen in this photo of B-29-1-BW, serial number 42-6242, the three-bladed propellers of the YB-29s had been replaced by four-bladed Hamilton Standard Hydromatic propellers with a diameter of 16 feet, 7 inches: 5 inches less than the three-bladed props.

A soldier stands next to B-29-1-BW, serial number 42-6242, for scale. Under the empennage is a retractable tail skid, which protected the rear of the fuselage from damage during nose-high landings and takeoffs. On the fuselage next to the forward part of the dorsal fin, an escape hatch over the auxiliary power unit is open. The auxiliary power unit (APU) was used for starting the engine and for supplying power to the aircraft and for emergency power; it was located in the unpressurized part of the aft fuselage.

Boeing B-29-1-BW, serial number 42-6242, is shown during an early flight. Note the RDF "football" antenna on the fuselage aft of the forward turret. After delivery to the Army on November 2, 1943, this plane was dispatched to the 794th Bombardment Squadron, 468th Bombardment Group, at Smoky Hill Army Air Field, Kansas.

A final photo of B-29-1-BW, serial number 42-6242, shows the plane in its early configuration with turrets installed. Later, this Superfortress would serve under the nickname "Esso Express" with the 468th Bombardment Group, ferrying fuel "over the Hump" from India to advanced USAAF bases in China. For that purpose, the turrets, armor, and other unnecessary gear were removed, and bomb-bay fuel tanks were installed.

The first of the production Superfortresses, B-29-1-BW, serial number 42-6205, is parked on a tarmac at an unidentified airfield around 1943–44. The turrets, except the tail turret, were not mounted, and a radome for the AN/APQ-13 radar set is present on the belly between the bomb bays. An extra antenna mast was mounted atop the fuselage, and a blind-landing antenna was between the RDF football antenna and the forward antenna mast.

Boeing B-29-1-BW, serial number 42-6246, takes off from an advanced airfield, with tents in the background, in the China-Burma-India (CBI) theater on May 10, 1944. A radome is visible between the main landing-gear wheels. While serving with the 679th Bombardment Squadron, 444th Bombardment Group, this plane crashed following the failure of engines 1 and 3 during a flight from Kharagpur, India, to Hsi Chang, China, on June 28, 1944; three crewmen were killed and eight survived. *National Archives*

An unidentified B-29 with turrets not mounted is parked at an airfield in China in 1944. Below and aft of the cockpit canopy is an SCR-729 antenna. A Yagi-type directional antenna, this was part of an airborne Rebecca transponding interrogator set, used in conjunction with a Eureka ground-based transponder for guiding the plane during an airfield approach.

Army Air Forces mechanics are working on engine number 1 on a B-29 at an advanced airfield. Bare aluminum on the leading edges of the wings and the empennage, where the deicer boots had been removed, was a common feature on the early, camouflage-painted B-29s.

"Pioneer," the fourth Boeing B-29-1-BW, serial number 42-6208, served with the 793rd Bombardment Squadron, 468th Bombardment Group, and arrived in India on September 23, 1944.

"Pepper," B-29-1-BW, serial number 42-6217, was assigned to the 762nd Bombardment Squadron, 468th Bombardment Group, in the CBI. In addition to nine bomb symbols, signifying bombing missions, below the cockpit canopy, there are numerous camel symbols on the nose, signifying "flying the Hump" missions over the Himalayas.

"Old Man Mose" was the nickname of B-29-1-BW, serial number 42-6209. To the rear of the head of the old man in the nose art is a cartoon balloon that reads "I'sa Comin." "Rollo" is painted below the open window in the canopy, and several faded camel and bomb symbols are below the front of the canopy. This Superfortress served with the 769th Bombardment Squadron, 462nd Bombardment Squadron, in the CBI before transferring to Tinian during April 1945.

The cowgirl nose art of a B-29 nicknamed "Cock-Sure" is viewed close-up. This is one of the very early Boeing-Wichita B-29s, with the Olive Drab over Neutral Gray camouflage paint.

The left parts of the engineer's panel and stand, as he faced them, are depicted, including oil temperature and pressure gauges, oil and fuel quantity indicators, and fire extinguisher controls.

One of the first officially released photos of the B-29 was this view in the rear part of the aft pressurized cabin, showing built-in, two-tiered cots on each side of the compartment for crewmen to rest on during long missions, thus reducing flight fatigue. The view is through the aft door of the pressurized compartment. This was an early configuration of the cots: soon, a radar operator's station would replace the cots on the left side.

In this B-29, the left cots in the aft pressurized compartment have been replaced by a radar operator's station, including a radarscope, an instrument panel, a desk, and other gear. The crewman to the left is in the aft, unpressurized compartment; to his rear, some of the exhaust line and plumbing of the auxiliary power unit, nicknamed the "putt-putt," are visible.

In addition to the bombardier, who doubled as the nose gunner, there were three gunners in the aft pressurized compartment: a top gunner, seen here seated at his station, and two side gunners. The top gunner was designated the central fire-control (CFC) gunner and served as the chief gunner. His seat rotated in unison with his gunsight, and he nominally controlled both top turrets, although there were numerous other combinations in which the gunners could control the various turrets.

As B-29 raids on Japan increased in frequency and volume, the Japanese adapted tactics of massed frontal attacks on B-29 bomber formations, which was an unexpected phenomenon. To better deal with such attacks, General Electric developed a top front turret with four instead of two .50-caliber machine guns. The two center machine guns were slightly higher than the outboard guns. Shown here is a four-gun top front turret being fired on the ground, with the fairing removed. The curved piece of metal on the rear of the turret ring worked in conjunction with a contour follower mounted between the barrels of the center machine guns to physically prevent the guns from shooting up features on the aircraft, such as the top of the fuselage and the empennage.

A woman worker poses in the left waist blister window of a B-29 as two workers operate on the vertical tail. The plane is in bare-aluminum finish, and black deicer boots are present on the leading edges of the dorsal fin and the horizontal stabilizer.

The lower forward turret of a B-29, armed with twin .50-caliber machine guns, is viewed facing aft. Aft of the turret, the doors of both bomb bays are open. The actuating arms on the front ends of the forward-bay doors are the early, electrically operated type, later replaced by pneumatic actuators. Inside that bomb bay is an auxiliary fuel tank.

Whereas the top, or CFC, gunner's sight was mounted on a ring and rotated in unison with the gunner's seat, the two waist gunners had pedestal-mounted retiflector gunsights. These sights operated through a fire-control computer to calculate deflection of the target. The sight's base had selsyn generators that transmitted electrical signals for azimuth and elevation to the turrets.

Armorers are operating on the tail turret of a B-29 at a base in India. The top of the ball of the turret and the fairing that seals off the joint between the rear of the fuselage and the ball of the turret have been removed. This was one of the tail turrets armed both with twin .50-caliber machine guns and a 20 mm cannon. Because of a disparity in the trajectories of the two types of weapons, they could be fired accurately together only at close ranges. Some models of the B-29 omitted the 20 mm cannon. *National Archives*

The first XB-29, the fourteen YB-29s, and the first forty B-29s produced by Boeing-Wichita were painted in the camouflage scheme of Olive Drab over Neutral Gray. Subsequent aircraft were issued in bare-aluminum finish, such as this example, Boeing B-29-25-BW, serial number 42-24464. Omitting the exterior paint saved weight and reduced drag. *National Archives*

Boeing B-29-30-BW, serial number 42-24473, flies above farmlands; note the open escape hatch on the fuselage next to the forward end of the dorsal fin. Most of the aluminum-alloy skin is highly reflective, but the skin on the fuselage section between the wings is of a dull finish. *National Archives*

Bombs are lined up in front of "Silver Lady," B-29-65-BW, serial number 44-69844, at an airfield in the Marianas. The forward top turret is the type armed with four .50-caliber machine guns instead of the original two guns. On the tail is the letter *E* in a circle symbol for the 504th Bombardment Group. *National Archives*

On November 24, 1944, US Army Engineer troops at Isley Field, Saipan, are witnessing the takeoff of a B-29 during the first US bombing mission against Tokyo since Jimmy Doolittle's small-scale raid on that city in April 1942. This raid was against the Nakajima aircraft factory. *National Archives*

Bell-Marietta B-29-25-BA, serial number 42-63529, *left,* from the 795th Bombardment Squadron (renumbered 794th in October 1944), 468th Bombardment Group, and another B-29 are raining down bombs on a Japanese airbase outside Rangoon, Burma.

As seen at an airfield on Okinawa in 1945, "Ready Teddy" was a Bell-Marietta B-29-30-BA, serial number 42-63561, assigned to the 5th Bombardment Squadron, 9th Bombardment Group, 313th Bombardment Wing. On the tail is the X-in-a-circle symbol of the 9th Bomb Group. Later, this plane received nose art of a bear to the rear of the "Ready Teddy" inscription.

A photographer documented the aftermath of the explosion of a B-29 named "Little Clambert" of the 40th Bombardment Group at Chakulia, India, on January 14, 1945. The remains of that plane are scattered in the foreground, while in the background is the heavily damaged B-29-10-BA nicknamed "Last Resort," serial number 42-63394, which was written off.

A local soldier armed with a rifle stands guard over Boeing B-29-10-BW, serial number 42-6340, at an airfield in the CBI. A cover is secured over the barrel of the 20 mm cannon in the tail turret. On the side of the turret is a light-colored panel with a window: this was an escape hatch. *National Archives*

Although airfoil-shaped radar antennas are generally associated with certain B-29Bs, at least one B-29 was fitted with such an apparatus, as seen in this color photograph of Bell-Marietta B-29-45-BA, serial number 44-83947.

"Sweat 'er Out" was the nickname of Bell-Marietta-built B-29-20-BA, serial number 42-63471, serving with the 871st Bombardment Squadron, 497th Bombardment Group, 73rd Bombardment Wing. According to the reminiscences of a crew member, the crew of the plane paid an airman/artist to execute the pinup art. *Air Force Historical Research Agency*

"The Ancient Mariner" was the nickname of B-29-25-MO, serial number 42-65296, assigned to the 883rd Bombardment Squadron, 500th Bombardment Group, based at Isley Field, Saipan, in May 1945. *Air Force Historical Research Agency*

"Nip Clipper," B-29-25-BA, serial number 42-63512, assigned to the 5th Bombardment Squadron, 9th Bombardment Group, was photographed on Tinian. On August 8, 1945, the plane was shot up over Yawata, Japan, during a bombing mission. The crew parachuted out over the Pacific; the plane commander, Lt. George Keller, was killed during his descent. They were picked up by the Japanese and were briefly detained as prisoners of war until the Japanese surrender.

Bell-Marietta B-29-25-BA, serial number 42-63508, was nicknamed "Peachy" by one of its pilots, Capt. Robert T. Haver, of the 482nd Bombardment Squadron, 505th Bombardment Group, 20th Air Force, based on Tinian. The plane was shot down and its crew perished over Tokyo during a nighttime incendiary bombing raid on May 25, 1945. A surviving B-29 at the Pueblo Weisbrod Aircraft Museum, Pueblo, Colorado, bears replica markings for Peachy. *Air Force Historical Research Agency*

"Oh Brother!" of the 411th Bombardment Squadron, 502nd Bombardment Group, was a B-29-30-BA. The plane is seen here with nose art of a happy Mickey Mouse lolling in a martini glass, likely on Guam in 1945.

The forward fuselage of the B-29 offered plenty of surface space for nose art, and the artist who painted the pinup art for "Lucky Lady" took full advantage of that "canvas." This was B-29-50-BW, serial number 42-24863, with the 504th Bombardment Group, 313th Bombardment Wing.

In a photo presumably taken at Isley Field, Saipan, a Wright R-3350 radial engine is hoisted on a portable crane alongside "Lady Mary Anna," B-29-40-BW, serial number 42-24625, from the 875th Bombardment Squadron, 498th Bombardment Group. The scoreboard on the fuselage includes seventeen bomb symbols, indicating combat missions, and one Japanese flag, indicating an aircraft kill.

A particularly imaginative scoreboard was on the left side of the forward fuselage of "Thumper," B-29-40-BW, serial number 42-24623, from the 870th Bombardment Squadron, 497th Bombardment Group. Each combat-mission symbol had a bomb with the target city's name on it; some also have Japanese flags, which indicate kills by the plane's gunners.

After completing forty combat missions, "Thumper" was flown back to the United States in order to visit airports in support of the US War Bonds program. This photo reportedly was taken at Boeing's Plant 2 at Seattle on August 7, 1945.

"Lil Organ Annie," Boeing B-29-50-BW, serial number 42-24893, of the 794th Bombardment Squadron, 468th Bombardment Group, 58th Bombardment Wing, 20th Air Force, bears the letter *I* in a triangle symbol of the 468th Bomb Group. This B-29 was delivered on November 30, 1944, and at the time this photo was taken, the plane was based at West Field, Tinian. The meaning of the star on the outboard engine nacelle is not known.

Although the cost of capturing Iwo Jima in February 1945 was very high, the island saved many B-29 aircrews who otherwise would have had to ditch their planes during the long treks to and from the airfields in the Marianas. Shown here is the first B-29 to make an emergency landing on Iwo Jima after its capture, B-29-25-MO, serial number 42-65286, with the X-over-triangle markings of the 9th Bombardment Group.

"Flak Alley Sally," Boeing B-29-55-BW, serial number 42-24878, has made an emergency landing at Iwo Jima's Motoyama Airfield No. 2 on March 17, 1945, following a raid on Kobe, Japan, the preceding night. The tail markings of an *L* over a triangle were those of the 6th Bombardment Group up to April 1945.

In a view taken from inside the nose of a B-29, two Superfortresses with the P-in-a-square symbol of the 39th Bombardment Group, 314th Bombardment Wing, are dropping bombs on a target. This specific marking dates the photograph to April 1945 or later.

Four B-29s from the 9th Bombardment Group, 313rd Bombardment Wing, fly in formation during a mission. The plane in the foreground is Victor number "55." The X-in-a-circle group symbol dated from April 1945.

As of this writing, there are only two airworthy B-29s remaining: one that goes by the nickname "Fifi," and, shown here, "Doc," Boeing B-29-70-BW, serial number 44-69972. Tony Mazzolini discovered the plane, mostly intact but in a severely deteriorated condition, in a remote area of the Naval Ordnance Test Station, China Lake, California, in 1987. Tony Mazzolini spearheaded the discovery, recovery, and restoration of the plane, which, after years of rebuilding, made its first flight since 1956 on July 17, 2016. *Rich Kolasa*

As restored, "Doc" lacks the top and bottom turrets but is equipped with a tail turret. The nose art features a cartoon likeness of "Doc," a character in the Disney movie *Snow White and the Seven Dwarfs. Rich Kolasa*

The nosewheels have cleared the runway as "Doc" takes off on a flight. The two white antennas on the top of the fuselage aft of the cockpit canopy are modern additions. Some of the aircrew members of "Doc" have been veterans of the Commemorative Air Force's B-29, "Fifi." *Rich Kolasa*

"Doc," Boeing B-29-70-BW, serial number 44-69972, was delivered to the Army Air Forces in March 1945 and did not see combat or overseas service. In the 1950s, the aircraft was converted to a TB-29 trainer. *Rich Kolasa*

The "Doc" restoration lacks markings aside from the nose art and nickname, the national insignia, the tail number, various stencils, and, below the horizontal tails, the inscription "B-29 SUPERFORTRESS" and the plane's civil registration number, N69972. *Rich Kolasa*

"Doc" is observed from the lower left quarter during flight. The aluminum-alloy skin of the airframe is highly polished and is evocative of a factory-fresh Superfortress. *Rich Kolasa*

The flaps are slightly lowered, the main landing-gear doors are open, and the nose-gear doors are closed in this in-flight photo of "Doc." *Rich Kolasa*

Boeing B-29-60-BW, serial number 44-69729, was a combat veteran, serving with the 875th Bombardment Squadron, 498th Bombardment Group, 73rd Bombardment Wing, and completing thirty-seven bombing missions in World War II. In 1949, the plane was converted to a KB-29 aerial-refueling tanker. After being recovered from the Naval Ordnance Test Station, China Lake, California, in 1986, the bomber was restored and was displayed at Lowry Air Force Base, Colorado, before being transferred to its current home, the Museum of Flight, in Seattle, Washington. *Tracy White*

Boeing B-29-60-BW, serial number 44-69729, is viewed from its left forward quarter, exhibiting details of the nose and canopy. The nose landing-gear doors on this plane are not present. *Tracy White*

The top forward turret of Boeing B-29-60-BW, serial number 44-69729, at the Museum of Flight, Seattle, is viewed from the left side. This is the four-gun version. Aft of the turret is the navigator's astrodome. Also in view is the navigator's window. *Tracy White*

The top forward turret, with four machine guns, is viewed from the left front, with the astrodome and the RDF "football" antenna to the rear. *Tracy White*

A top forward four-gun turret is viewed from the right side. On the fuselage below the turret are two white feed-through insulators for the command and liaison wire radio antennas. Also in view is the flight engineer's window / escape hatch. *Tracy White*

The forward lower turret of B-29-60-BW, serial number 44-69729, exhibits two .50-caliber machine guns. Ejector ports for spent cartridges are on the bottom of the gun shield. *Tracy White*

The same forward lower turret is observed from the left side of the fuselage. The nose landing-gear bay with its missing doors is to the upper left, and the nacelles for engines number 3 and 4 are in the background. *Tracy White*

Another view of the same forward lower turret shows the front of the unit, facing toward the rear of the fuselage. Aft of the turret is a radome. *Tracy White*

The radome located between the bomb bays is viewed from the side. *Tracy White*

The clear Plexiglas dome for the CFC gunner and, to its rear, the top aft turret are viewed from the right side of the fuselage of a B-29. In the foreground is the door, with two recessed latch handles, for the right life-raft compartment; a similar door and compartment are on the opposite side of the fuselage. *Tracy White*

The top aft turret and the CFC gunner's Plexiglas dome are on the top of the fuselage, as seen from the right side. To the lower right is part of the right waist gunner's clear sighting dome. *Tracy White*

The CFC gunner's clear dome, the top aft turret, and the left waist gunner's clear dome are seen from the left side of the fuselage. Inside the waist gunner's dome is the pedestal gunsight. *Tracy White*

The CFC gunner's dome and the top aft turret are viewed close-up. The dome of the turret rests on a fairing that is riveted to the fuselage. *Tracy White*

The lower aft turret of a B-29 is seen from the right side. On the bottom of the gun shield are four ejector ports. The larger, outboard ones are for spent cartridge casings, and the smaller, inboard ones are for cartridge links. *Tracy White*

The lower aft turret is viewed from the right side, with the left horizontal stabilizer visible to the lower left. *Tracy White*

Boeing B-29-75-BW, serial number 44-70016, is on static display at the Pima Air & Space Museum, in Tucson, Arizona. It is a combat veteran of World War II, having served under the nickname "Sentimental Journey" with the 458th Bombardment Squadron, 330th Bombardment Group, based at North Field on Guam. From 1954 until its retirement in 1959, it served with the 4713th Radar Evaluation Squadron at Griffiss Air Force Base in New York. In 1969, the plane was removed from storage at Davis-Monthan Air Force Base, Tucson, and became part of the collection of the US Air Force Museum until sent on loan to the Pima Air & Space Museum. "Quaker City" artwork is on the right side of the forward fuselage, and flight crew and ground crew names are marked on the nose. *Author photo*

The forward left portion of "Sentimental Journey," including the nickname, is displayed. Painted in yellow with thin black outlining on the bottom of the nose is "K40K." The names of additional ground crewmen and the armorers are painted on the side of the nose. *Author photo*

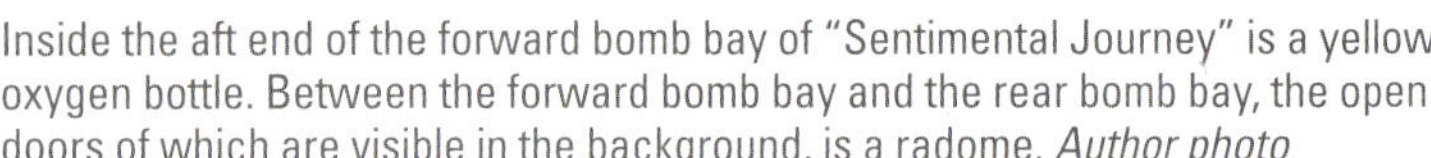
Inside the aft end of the forward bomb bay of "Sentimental Journey" is a yellow oxygen bottle. Between the forward bomb bay and the rear bomb bay, the open doors of which are visible in the background, is a radome. *Author photo*

The forward end of the aft bomb bay is shown, with the radome and the open doors of the forward bomb bay in the background. At the top is the communications tunnel between the forward and aft pressurized compartments. Below the tunnel is the rear of the wing structure that passes through the fuselage, below which are the pneumatic bomb-bay door actuators, which caused the doors to snap open immediately. *Author photo*

A view up into one of the bomb bays includes the communications tunnel and a yellow oxygen bottle (*top*) and two of the bomb racks. The communications tunnel was necessary for crewmen to pass back and forth from the forward and aft pressurized compartments, because the bomb bays were not pressurized. *Author photo*

The right rear of "Sentimental Journey" is shown. The numeral "4" in the number "40" overlaps the aft crew door. A ladder, one of which was provided for each B-29, was necessary for using this door when the plane was parked on ground. On the tail is the K-in-a-square symbol of the 330th Bombardment Group. *Author photo*

CHAPTER 4

The Silverplate Bombers

As the scientists at Los Alamos labored to create the world's first nuclear weapons, one of the considerations was how such weapons were to be delivered. This question was made even more challenging as a result of two types of nuclear devices that were developed—"Thin Man" and "Fat Man"; the former, which was 17 feet long, was proven to be unworkable, and a new style of weapon, code name "Little Boy," was devised.

Early on, brief consideration was given to using a B-24 Liberator as a delivery mechanism, but that idea was quickly discarded for a variety of reasons. Next, the Avro Lancaster was considered, even to the extent of consulting the aircraft's chief designer, Roy Chadwick. Shown only a sketch of the two bomb casings, Chadwick assured the US representative that the Lancaster could handle the job.

However, Gen. H. H. Arnold was not pleased with the idea of using a British aircraft to deliver America's new wonder weapon, and provided the authorization to take whatever steps were necessary to use a B-29 for the project.

As the United States' Manhattan Project readied the first atomic bombs in the latter part of World War II, the Army Air Forces set about preparing a force of B-29s equipped to carry the weapons to the enemy. Code-named "Silverplate," these Superfortresses were equipped with Wright R-3350-41 fuel-injected engines and Curtiss Electric reversible-pitch propellers. The upper and lower turrets were removed and their openings faired over, and other modifications were made to adapt the planes to their atomic mission. The most famous of the Silverplate B-29s was ""Enola Gay,"" B-29-45-MO, serial number 44-86292, named after the mother of Col. Paul W. Tibbets, the plane commander as well as the commander of the 509th Composite Group, the top-secret force of atomic bombers. The plane is shown here with tail markings for the 6th Bombardment Group, part of the deception measures taken to mask the true purpose of the Silverplate B-29s.

B-29 serial number 42-6259 was sent to Wright Field to be modified as a test article for carrying the weapons, which included linking the B-29's two bomb bays into a single large bomb bay, with two 27-foot bomb bay doors used rather than four 12-foot doors. The aircraft arrived at Muroc Field (now Edwards Air Force Base), California, for testing on February 20, 1944. The aircraft was used to test assorted variations in the shapes and tail fins of the bombs.

The modification of 42-6259 and subsequent atom-capable bombers were given the code name Silverplate. Project 98146-S was the first group of twenty-four series-modified atom-capable bombers ordered from the Martin Modification Center in Omaha. The first three were to be delivered by September 30, 1944, with eleven more by the end of the year and the remaining ten to come as soon as possible thereafter.

In February, Project 98228-S called for an additional twenty-four aircraft, since the rigorous training schedule was wearing out the original group. In April, five more aircraft were added to the order, with thirteen of them to be delivered before. These aircraft were to include the latest in development of the B-29 and, beyond the enlarged bomb bay, additionally differed from standard B-29s in having fuel-injected Wright R-3350-41 engines and Curtiss Electric reversible-pitch propellers, and in the deletion of the upper and lower turrets and much of the armor plate. The second group of Silverplate bombers would be the ones to go overseas with the 509th Composite Group and deliver the atomic weapons to Hiroshima and Nagasaki.

The modifications and improvements to the aircraft required extensive work, averaging 3,469 man-hours per aircraft. Further refinements of the design raised this to 11,000 man-hours per bomber.

The forward fuselage of "Enola Gay" is seen from the left side at around the time the plane dropped the first atomic bomb, on Hiroshima on August 6, 1945. Tibbets assumed command of the plane at North Field on Tinian, in the Marianas Islands, on August 5, the day before the first atomic-bombing mission, and at the same time he had the nickname painted on the aircraft. *Stan Piet collection*

After the first atomic-bombing mission, the inscription "First Atomic Bomb / Hiroshima—August 6, 1945," was painted on the right side of the forward fuselage of "Enola Gay."

Col. Paul W. Tibbets, *center*, poses with six members of the 509th Composite Group. His crew for the atomic mission on August 6, 1945, consisted of himself and eleven other men. *Air Force Historical Research Agency*

By the time this photo of "Enola Gay" was taken, the plane was back in the United States. On the forward fuselage is the insignia of the 509th Composite Group: specifically, the insignia as it was configured after the 509th was assigned to the 58th Bombardment Wing (Very Heavy) in 1946. *Stan Piet collection*

In the second atomic strike on Japan, against Nagasaki on August 9, 1945, the nuclear device, nicknamed "Fat Man," was dropped by "Bockscar," B-29-35-MO, serial number 44-27297. The nose art featured a flying boxcar over a railroad track spanning from Salt Lake City (*right*; located near Wendover Air Force Base, the original headquarters of the 509th Composite Group) to Nagasaki (*left*). *Stan Piet collection*

This grainy photograph of "Bockscar" in flight is believed to have been taken after the August 9, 1945, atomic mission, since the nose art, which is thought to have been applied after that mission, is present. For deceptive purposes, the N-in-a-triangle symbol of the 444th Bombardment Group is on the tail. A radome is present on the belly, and the plane's identifier (or Victor) number, "77," is on the aft fuselage.

"Up an' Atom," B-29-35-MO, serial number 44-27304, was the aircraft of Crew B-10 of the 393rd Bombardment Squadron, 509th Composite Group. Its Victor number was "88" at the time of the Hiroshima and Nagasaki attacks. The scoreboard below the cockpit canopy includes five black "fat-man" symbols, representing bombing missions against Japan using pumpkin bombs: conventional, high-explosive bombs with the same weight, shape, and ballistics as the Fat Man nuclear bomb, used for training the flight crews of the 509th Composite Group. The red fat-man symbol indicated a nuclear-bombing mission: the flight crew of "Up an' Atom" flew "Enola Gay" on the Nagasaki mission as the weather aircraft for the primary target that day, Kokura. *Stan Piet collection*

Another Silverplate bomber with the 393rd Bombardment Squadron, 509th Composite Group, was "Strange Cargo," B-29-35-MO, serial number 44-27300, and Victor number "73." Crew A-4 was assigned to this plane. *Stan Piet collection*

"Full House," B-29-35-MO, serial number 44-27298, Victor number "83," was assigned to Crew A-1 of the 393rd Bombardment Squadron, 509th Composite Group, and participated in the Hiroshima strike as a weather plane; it was assigned as a backup bomber for the Nagasaki attack. *Stan Piet collection*

Closely related to the outhouse theme of the nose art "Full House" was the Silverplate bomber nicknamed "Straight Flush," B-29-35-MO, serial number 44-27301, and Victor number 85, assigned to the 393rd Bombardment Squadron, 509th Composite Group. "Straight Flush" served as a weather-reconnaissance plane on the Hiroshima atomic mission. *Stan Piet collection*

B-29-35-MO, serial number 44-27296, of Silverplate, was nicknamed "Some Punkins," a reference to the pumpkin bombs the 509th Composite Group used against Japan in preparation for the August 1945 atomic strikes. This plane's Victor number was "84." *Stan Piet collection*

One of the most famous aircraft in history, "Enola Gay," has had the good fortune to be preserved by the Smithsonian Institution since 1949, in an era when countless other significant aircraft were allowed to deteriorate or were sent to the wrecker's yard. After many years of storage outdoors at Andrews Air Force Base, Maryland, the plane was disassembled and placed in storage in the Paul E. Garber Facility, where technicians gradually reassembled and restored the bomber. Once again intact, "Enola Gay" is exhibited at the National Air and Space Museum, Steven F. Udvar-Hazy Center. *Author photo*

Below the second window from the rear on the left side of "Enola Gay"'s canopy is a red stencil that reads "CUT THRU GLASS FOR EMERGENCY RESCUE." The black stencil at the center of the photo provides the plane's project number, DOM. 98289S; its nomenclature, "U.S. ARMY B-29 BLOCK 45 MO"; its maximum crew weights; and fuel specifications ("GRADE 130 . . . SUITABLE FOR AROMATICS"). *Author photo*

The cockpit canopy and clear nose of "Enola Gay" are viewed from the upper left. The Norden bombsight is visible through the clear nose. *Author photo*

In a close-up view of the canopy from the left side, the pilot's and copilot's seats are visible; in the background, visible through the upper window, are the flight engineer's instrument panel and control stand. *Author photo*

The fuselage and parts of the wings and engine number 3 are viewed from the nose. The flatness of the bomb-aiming window on the front of the clear nose is apparent. *Author photo*

In a photo of the forward fuselage, the names and ranks of the members of the "Enola Gay" flight crew on the Hiroshima atomic mission are stenciled below the second window from the rear. At the center of the photograph is the engineer's window, which also was designed as an escape hatch. *Author photo*

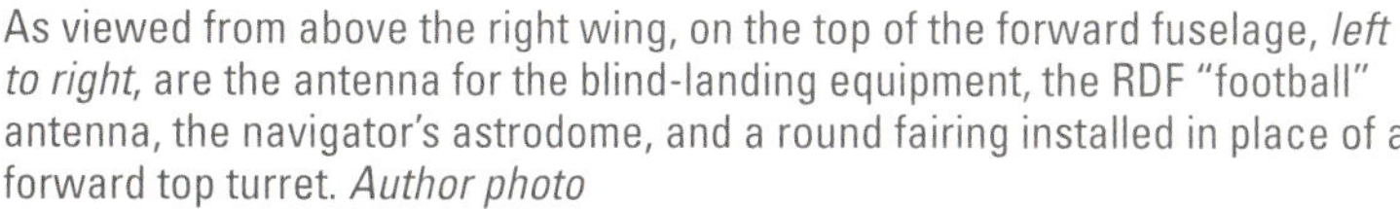

As viewed from above the right wing, on the top of the forward fuselage, *left to right*, are the antenna for the blind-landing equipment, the RDF "football" antenna, the navigator's astrodome, and a round fairing installed in place of a forward top turret. *Author photo*

The nacelle and cowling for engine number 4, *foreground*, and part of the nacelle and cowling for engine number 3 are observed. Curtiss Electric four-bladed propellers with cooling cuffs on the blades are installed. Ventilating louvers and the flight hood, through which engine exhaust was expelled after being used to propel the turbosupercharger, are on the sides of the nacelles. *Author photo*

The light-colored panel on the darker-colored skin on the fuselage between the wings is the door for the right life-raft compartment. Two recessed lock handles are on the door. *Author photo*

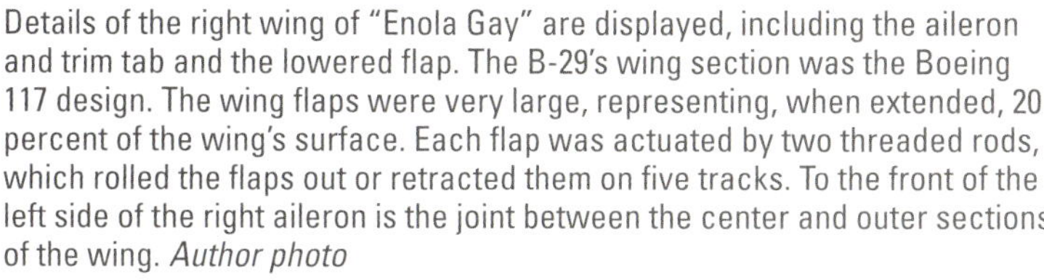

Details of the right wing of "Enola Gay" are displayed, including the aileron and trim tab and the lowered flap. The B-29's wing section was the Boeing 117 design. The wing flaps were very large, representing, when extended, 20 percent of the wing's surface. Each flap was actuated by two threaded rods, which rolled the flaps out or retracted them on five tracks. To the front of the left side of the right aileron is the joint between the center and outer sections of the wing. *Author photo*

The right wingtip is viewed from above. A clear, form-fitting lens is installed over the green navigation light on the leading edge of the wingtip. *Author photo*

The tail of "Enola Gay" is viewed from the right side, showing details of the design of the rudder, the dorsal fin, and the tail turret. Although the upper and lower turrets were omitted from the "Enola Gay" during its production, the tail turret remained in place. *Author photo*

"Enola Gay" currently wears the R-in-a-circle tail symbol it used after arriving on Tinian prior to the Hiroshima strike. This symbol was the one used by the 6th Bombardment Group on Tinian and was applied to "Enola Gay" as a security precaution. *Author photo*

In a photo of the left side of the empennage of "Enola Gay," the angular construction of the forward part of the rudder is apparent. *Author photo*

Because no upper and lower turrets were installed on "Enola Gay," the sighting blisters also were omitted, and the openings for them were covered with aluminum-alloy fairings. The fairings at the waist positions had small, round windows in the centers. *Author photo*

The radome on the belly of the fuselage between the forward and aft bomb bays is viewed from the left side facing aft. *Author photo*

"Bockscar," B-29-36-MO, serial number 44-27297, which dropped the Fat Man atomic bomb on Nagasaki, Japan, on August 9, 1945, has been preserved. The plane returned to the United States in November 1945, and in the following year the title to the plane was transferred to the Air Force Museum (now the National Museum of the United States Air Force) at Wright-Patterson Air Force Base, Ohio, where the restored aircraft remains on display. The nose art as seen in this photo is a reproduction. *Author photo*

Details of the nose landing gear and forward fuselage of "Bockscar" are exhibited. Mounted on the front of the nose shock strut above the dual wheels are a shimmy damper and a centering cam and cover. On the rear of the shock strut is the torsion link, sometimes called the antitorque link.

This nearly overall view of "Bockscar" provides a clear impression of the massive size of the wing flaps, seen here in their raised positions. The Boeing 117 Wing had several advantages, including decreased drag per pound of lift, improved stall warning and more-gradual stalling characteristics, and a maximized interspar area, which allowed more room for wing fuel tanks while also increasing the strength of the wing.

The forward bomb bay of "Bockscar" is viewed facing aft, with the crew communications tunnel above, bomb racks to the sides, and the front of the wing structure in the background. The tunnel had an upward jog in it to accommodate the shape of the Fat Man nuclear bomb carried in this aircraft to Nagasaki in August 1945.

The fairing over the opening left where the sighting blister for the left waist gunner of "Bockscar" is, on the side of the fuselage next to the national insignia. *Author photo*

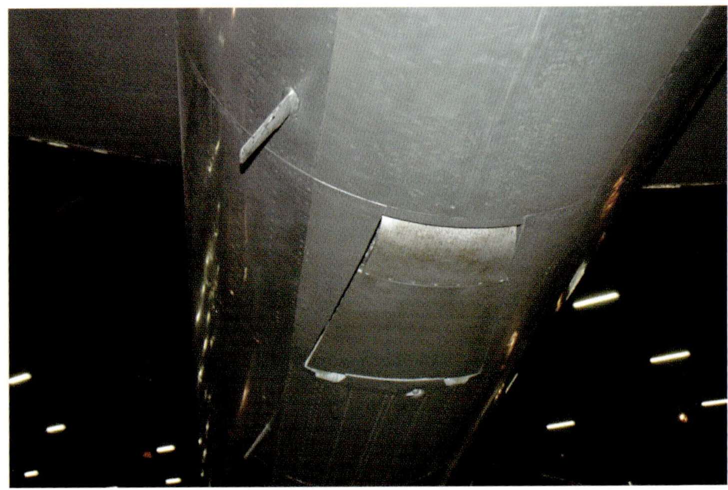

The tail skid of "Bockscar" is in its retracted position on the bottom of the aft fuselage. *Author photo*

Details worthy of notice on the tail turret of "Bockscar" include the canvas boot to seal off the rear of the ball part of the turret, below which is the spent-casing ejector chute. *Author photo*

The flight deck of "Bockscar" includes a mannequin in a flight suit seated at the bombardier's station in the nose. Note the different layouts of the airplane commander's (or pilot's; *left*) and copilot's main instrument panels, and the locations of the control pedestals on the outboard sides of the control columns. In the center foreground is the aisle stand.

The aircraft commander's station is shown in detail. The logo plate on the hub of the steering wheel was a prized souvenir and often came up missing. The large wheel on the side of the control pedestal is the elevator tabs control. On the pedestal were throttle controls and lock and other controls. Below the main instrument panel are rudder pedals.

The copilot's instrument panel was more spare than the aircraft commander's. The control pedestal mimicked the aircraft commander's, with the addition of a radio-compass control box to the rear of the throttle controls.

The engineer's instrument panel and stand in "Bockscar" are in a remarkable state of preservation. On the stand, to the right are fuel mixture (*orange*) controls and lock and throttle controls (*blue*), while on the left side of the stand are controls for cabin air (*white*) and vacuum pump selector (*gray*). On the far left of the stand are slots for two fuel-tank selector levers, which are missing.

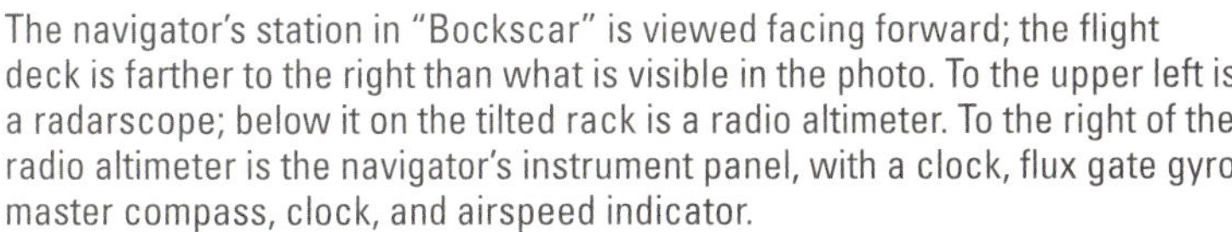

The navigator's station in "Bockscar" is viewed facing forward; the flight deck is farther to the right than what is visible in the photo. To the upper left is a radarscope; below it on the tilted rack is a radio altimeter. To the right of the radio altimeter is the navigator's instrument panel, with a clock, flux gate gyro master compass, clock, and airspeed indicator.

The radio operator's compartment, as seen in "Bockscar," was aft of the flight engineer's station. A command receiver and other radio sets are on the upper rack. On the table at the center of the photo is a liaison receiver set. The radio operator's station did not have a window.

CHAPTER 5

B-29A

Functionally and dimensionally, the B-29A was identical to the basic B-29. The B-29A designation indicated a different type of wing center structure. While the B-29 had a two-piece wing center section that bolted together in the middle and supported the engine nacelles, the B-29A used a single, shorter center section that did not extend beyond the sides of the fuselage. To this center section were attached short sections of wing including the nacelles, and outboard of that were the outer wing panels. The outer wing panels themselves were identical to those on the B-29.

While the B-29 was built by Boeing-Wichita, Bell-Marietta, and Martin-Omaha, the B-29A was produced solely at the Boeing-Renton plant. During the course of production, an improved, more streamlined forward upper turret housing was introduced at production block 40. The first Renton-built Superfortress flew on December 30, 1943, and the final B-29A rolled out of the Renton plant on June 10, 1946. In the interim, a total of 1,119 B-29As were produced.

Produced solely at Boeing's Renton, Washington, facility, the B-29As differed from the B-29 primarily in the design of the wings. Whereas the B-29's wings consisted of a two-piece center section that was bolted together along the plane's longitudinal centerline, with outer wing sections attached to the center section outboard of the outer engine nacelles, the B-29A had a single-piece center wing section with no center joint, to which were joined two wing sections, each of which contained two engine nacelles, with outer wing sections attached on the outboard sides of the outer nacelles. Shown here is the first B-29A-1-BN ("BN" standing for Boeing-Renton), serial number 42-93824, positioned on portable scales to calculate the aircraft's weight.

B-29A Serial Numbers

Production block	Starting serial number	Ending serial number
B-29A-1-BN	42-93824	42-93843
B-29A-5-BN	42-93844	42-93873
B-29A-10-BN	42-93874	42-93923
B-29A-15-BN	42-93924	42-93973
B-29A-20-BN	42-93974	42-94023
B-29A-25-BN	42-94024	42-94073
B-29A-30-BN	42-94074	42-94123
B-29A-35-BN	44-61510	44-61609
B-29A-40-BN	44-61610	44-61709
B-29A-45-BN	44-61710	44-61809
B-29A-50-BN	44-61810	44-61909
B-29A-55-BN	44-61910	44-62009
B-29A-60-BN	44-62010	44-62109
B-29A-65-BN	44-62110	44-62209
B-29A-70-BN	44-62210	44-62309
B-29A-75-BN	44-62310	44-62328

Workmen are preparing a B-29A-5-BN for delivery to the Army. The nomenclature and data stencil below the cockpit canopy make it clear this is a B-29A-5-BN; below that line, the third from last digit of the serial number is difficult to read, but by process of elimination it is 42-93855, which makes it the first B-29A-5-BN.

Under tow along the water outside the Boeing-Renton plant is B-29A-10-BN, serial number 42-93888. At first, B-29As had to be barged from this plant across the Cedar River to the Renton Airport, from which they were delivered. Later, a bridge was built across the river to accommodate aircraft.

Boeing B-29A-30-BN, serial number 42-94106, is devoid of markings except for the national insignia and the tail number. The forward top turret is the four-gun type, and the tail turret is armed with two .50-caliber machine guns, the 20 mm cannon having been omitted by then.

Boeing B-29A-5-BN, serial number 42-93869, was delivered on September 16, 1944. Subsequently, it was converted to an F-13A long-distance photoreconnaissance plane and assigned to the 3rd Photographic Reconnaissance Squadron, 311th Photographic Reconnaissance Wing. The plane crashed and was damaged beyond repair, with no crew fatalities, during a takeoff from Guam on April 26, 1945.

Seen in a predelivery flight is B-29A-30-BN, serial number 42-94106. The aft crew door appears as a light-colored rectangle aft of the national insignia on the fuselage.

A late-type, four-gun forward top turret was developed for the B-29, featuring a streamlined dome and a fairing that matched the contours of the turret dome when positioned at 0 degrees azimuth. The turret is on a B-29A-75-BN, with the insignia of the 25th Bombardment Squadron featured prominently on the forward fuselage. *Stan Piet collection*

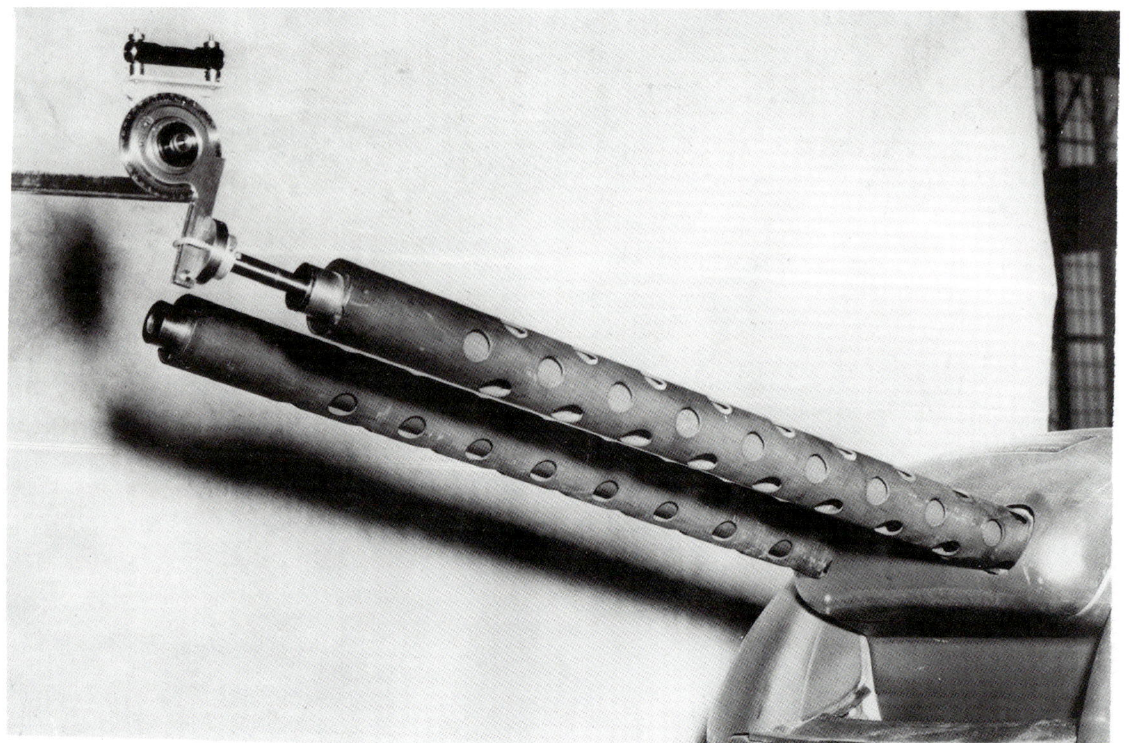

A July 5, 1945, photograph from General Electric, the designer and producer of the B-29's CFC system, documents a target-aligning level assembly, inserted in the barrel of the left gun in a B-29. This device was used for harmonizing the machine guns with the sights.

A lower aft turret from a B-29 is shown dismounted from the aircraft and with the dome removed. Ammunition boxes are on holders above the turret. The photo was taken on January 31, 1944, to illustrate a modification whereby an air hose was disconnected from the turret.

The same lower aft turret depicted in the preceding photo is viewed from the right rear, showing the rears of the receivers of the .50-caliber machine guns below the turret ring.

Bombs are loaded on racks inside a B-29 from the 314th Bombardment Wing at North Field on Guam on April 13, 1945. These appear to be M47 100-pound incendiary bombs, which came in chemical smoke or incendiary versions.

Boeing-Renton B-29A-60-BN, serial number 44-62070, which operates under the nickname "Fifi," is one of only two airworthy Superfortresses remaining, the other being "Doc," Boeing B-29-70-BW serial number 44-69972. After delivery, the Superfortress that became "Fifi" was converted to a TB-29A trainer. The plane was languishing at the US Naval Weapons Center, China Lake, California, when the Confederate Air Force (CAF: now Commemorative Air Force) acquired it in 1971. The CAF restored the plane to flying condition, and it continues to perform around the country in air shows and motion-picture production. *Rich Kolasa*

“Fifi” is viewed off its forward right quarter with engines running. The current power plants in this aircraft were custom built from Wright R-3350-95W and R-3350-26WD engines. *Rich Kolasa*

The flight engineer’s window / escape hatch and the aft crew door are open in this photo of “Fifi” in flight. Aft of the national insignia on the fuselage is the emblem of the Commemorative Air Force. *Rich Kolasa*

A study of the few available photos of "Fifi" taken at China Lake before it was recovered in 1971 indicates that at least the two top turrets and the forward lower turret lacked at least their domes, although the fairings for the turrets were intact on the fuselage. Installation of turrets, including a four-gun upper forward turret, were part of the restoration process. *Rich Kolasa*

The A-in-a-square group symbol on the tail of "Fifi" is not based on any historical bombardment group symbol from World War II. *Rich Kolasa*

"Fifi" is observed from the right rear during flight. The light-colored object protruding from the upper part of the dorsal fin is nonoriginal equipment and presumably is an antenna. *Rich Kolasa*

Nosewheel partially retracted, "Fifi" flies low over an airport. *Rich Kolasa*

"Fifi" taxis at an airport, still presenting a sleek, modern appearance almost three-quarters of a century after leaving the Boeing-Renton assembly line. *Rich Kolasa*

The lower aft turret of "Fifi" is seen close-up, looking forward. The gun barrels are facsimiles of those used on the original Browning .50-caliber machine guns. *Author photo*

The lower turret is viewed from underneath, including details of the fairing for the turret, which is attached to the fuselage with Phillips screws. *Author photo*

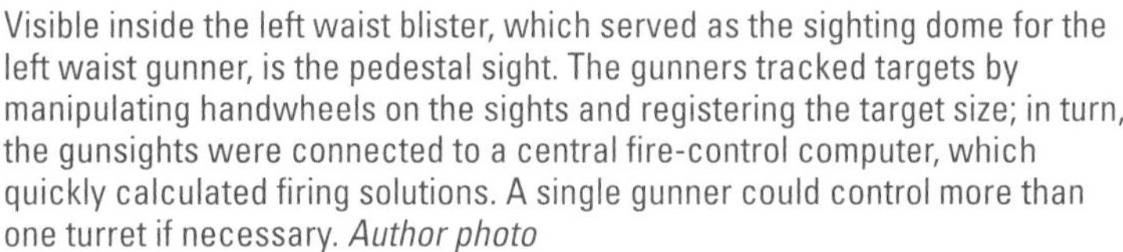

Visible inside the left waist blister, which served as the sighting dome for the left waist gunner, is the pedestal sight. The gunners tracked targets by manipulating handwheels on the sights and registering the target size; in turn, the gunsights were connected to a central fire-control computer, which quickly calculated firing solutions. A single gunner could control more than one turret if necessary. *Author photo*

The right waist blister is shown; the right pedestal sight is visible inside. *Author photo*

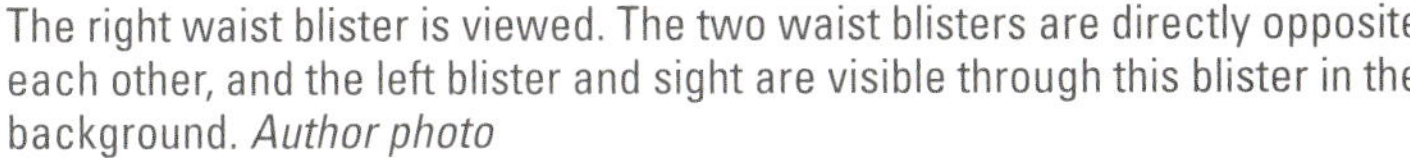

The right waist blister is viewed. The two waist blisters are directly opposite each other, and the left blister and sight are visible through this blister in the background. *Author photo*

The tail gunner, too, had a pedestal sight, and this is visible through the flat rear window of the tail turret. The round object on the rear of the roof, above the flat rear window, is the bomb formation light, also called the bomb release light, which was used to signal crews of following aircraft when the bombs were about to be released. *Author photo*

The rear window of the rear turret, the upper part of the gunsight, and the bomb formation light are observed close-up. *Author photo*

With the cowling and propeller of one of the Wright R-3500 radial engines of "Fifi" removed, the gear-reduction case, cylinders, ignition harness, and exhaust manifold are visible. *Rich Kolasa*

A surviving but not flightworthy Superfortress is this B-29A-60-BN, built by Boeing-Renton and accepted in July 1945. It is a composite of two aircraft: from the trailing edge of the wing forward is B-29A-55-BN, serial number 44-61975, while the remainder of the airframe was grafted on from B-29A-45-BN, serial number 44-61739. Both airframes were recovered from Aberdeen Proving Ground, Maryland, in the 1970s. The resulting aircraft is known as "Jack's Hack" and is on display at the New England Air Museum, Windsor Locks, Connecticut. *Rich Kolasa*

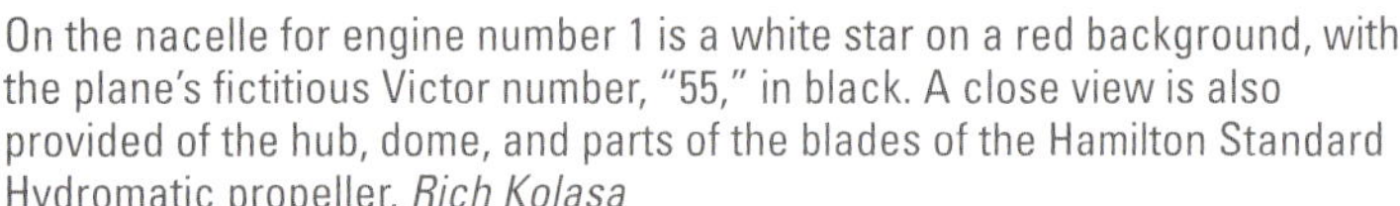

On the nacelle for engine number 1 is a white star on a red background, with the plane's fictitious Victor number, "55," in black. A close view is also provided of the hub, dome, and parts of the blades of the Hamilton Standard Hydromatic propeller. *Rich Kolasa*

The nose landing gear of "Jack's Hack" is pictured. *Rich Kolasa*

"Jack's Hack" is observed from the rear of the left wing, showing the open bomb-bay doors, the left main landing-gear and gear-bay doors, and the contours of the trailing edge of the wing. *Rich Kolasa*

The left main landing gear is viewed from a closer perspective, showing the dual tires and the torsion link on the lower rear of the oleo strut. Note the lightening hole on the upper part of the torsion link. *Rich Kolasa*

In another view from the left side of the aft fuselage, to the far right is part of the lower tail turret. The left waist sighting blister is on the side of the fuselage, and a radome is located between the two bomb bays. *Rich Kolasa*

The spatial relationship of the left sighting blister, the top sighting blister for the CFC gunner, and the top aft turret is displayed. *Rich Kolasa*

The lower aft turret is viewed from the left side; it is traversed aft. Perforated cooling jackets are fitted over the .50-caliber machine gun barrels. *Rich Kolasa*

The tail skid of "Jack's Hack" is lowered, as seen from the left side of the fuselage. The skid was lowered and retracted by the actuator on the rear of the skid. *Rich Kolasa*

The left side of the empennage of "Jack's Hack" is depicted, showing the position of the lowered tail skid. *Rich Kolasa*

The tail turret on "Jack's Hack" originally was on "Doc," Boeing B-29-70-BW, serial number 44-69972, depicted earlier in this book. In exchange for that tail turret, the vertical fin of "Jack's Hack" was given to "Doc" so that that plane could have a more airworthy fin, and a replacement fin was found for "Jack's Hack." *Rich Kolasa*

CHAPTER 6

B-29B

As the war against Japan wore on, and with the Allies controlling the air, the US bombing strategy evolved as well. The B-29B was optimized for use in the revised campaign.

The B-29B was produced solely by Bell at their Marietta, Georgia, facility. The aircraft lacked the two upper and two lower turrets, and the associated fire control system. The tail armament, consisting of a pair of .50-caliber machine guns and an M2 20 mm cannon, was retained. These weapons were controlled by an AN/APG-15B radar fire control system. The AN/APG-15 was an S-band radar system, code name Wasp, which detected and engaged enemy aircraft approaching from the rear. Once in the field, the troublesome 20 mm cannon was often removed, sometimes being replaced by a third .50-caliber machine gun.

The deletion of the heavy GE turrets and the associated fire control system, as well as the reduction of the crew by one man, considerably reduced the weight of the aircraft. As a result, performance was improved, with top speed increasing to 364 mph at 25,000 feet. The aircraft were also equipped with fast-acting, pneumatically operated bomb bay doors.

These aircraft were especially configured for high-level radar-guided bombing. Central to this was the APQ-7 "Eagle" radar bombing system. The 16-foot antenna for this system was housed in an 18-foot-long airfoil-shaped structure suspended beneath the B-29B central wing. The APQ-7 was the key component of the synchronous radar bombing system. With this system, the radar bombardier, whose position was in the navigator's compartment, tracked the target by using a reticle on the radar scope, which was linked to the Norden bombsight. As a result, the radar scope displayed a track to fly, ground speed, and time for bomb release. This information was also displayed in the cockpit on the pilot's direction indicator. The pilot engaged the autopilot, which held the aircraft straight and level.

Only 311 B-29Bs were built, all delivered between January and September 1945. The primary user of the B-29B was the 315th Bomb Wing, which began operations against Japan on June 26, 1945.

Produced solely by Bell-Marietta, the B-29B was a lightened version of the Superfortress, with all turrets but the tail one removed, along with the heavy General Electric fire-control computer and related equipment. It was possible to remove the turrets because by this time in World War II, threats from Japanese fighters tended to be solely from the aft quarter of the bombers. There also was a reduction in crew members. Some B-29Bs were equipped with the Western Electric AN/APQ-7 Eagle X-band targeting radar system, which featured a very distinctive airfoil-shaped antenna mounted on streamlined struts below the fuselage, as seen in a photo of an unidentified B-29B from the 16th Bombardment Group, 315th Bombardment Wing. *Stan Piet collection*

The undersides of some B-29Bs were painted in a glossy black at the Bell-Marietta factory, to make the aircraft less visible from ground gunners and spotters during nighttime bombing missions. Such a camouflage scheme is seen on this unidentified B-29B with the L-in-a-circle tail symbol of the 331st Bombardment Group, 315th Bombardment Wing. Red dustcovers are installed in the chin scoops of the cowlings. The sign to the front of the plane reads "NO SMOKING WITHIN 50FT OF PLANES." *Stan Piet collection*

"Lovely Leta," B-29B-45-BA, serial number 44-83959, and Victor number "53," of the 430th Bombardment Squadron, 502nd Bombardment Group, is taxiing at Northwest Field, Guam, in the summer of 1945. A comparison of the black camouflage paint on this B-29B with that in the preceding photo demonstrates the variations in the upper border of the paint as applied at the Bell-Marietta plant. The twin .50-caliber machine guns in the tail turret were automatically controlled by the AN/APG-15B radar fire-control system, the ball-shaped radar pod of which is visible below the .50-caliber machine gun barrels of the tail turret. Also present between the bomb bays is the antenna of an Eagle targeting radar. *Stan Piet collection*

A B-29B approaches the runway at North Field on Guam toward the end of World War II. Under the fuselage is the antenna of an AN/APQ-7 Eagle X-band targeting-radar system. Faintly visible on the tail is the symbol of the 16th Bombardment Group, 315th Bombardment Wing. This bomb wing was the only one to be fully equipped with the Eagle targeting radars, using them in bombing missions only in the final month of the war against Japan, but with impressive effectiveness. *San Diego Air & Space Museum*

Although taken around January 1948, a few years beyond the time frame of this book, it is included because it is an unusually clear photo of the antenna pod for the AN/APG-15B radar fire-control system that operated the tail turret. Lt. Col. Dale Seeds, director of a training program at the US Air Force base at Dharan, Saudi Arabia, is explaining the radar-controlled turret to a group of Saudi trainees. *National Archives*

A Bell-Marietta B-29B with the AN/APQ-7 Eagle radar is taking off on a mission from a base in the Marianas. On the tail is the Y-in-a-diamond symbol of the 501st Bombardment Group, 315th Bombardment Wing. *National Archives via Alan Griffith*

A B-29B with black camouflage on the bottom and tail marking for the 16th Bombardment Group, 315th Bombardment Wing, comes in for a landing in the Marianas in the final part of World War II. The camouflage has a slightly irregular but nonwavy upper border. An AN/APQ-7 Eagle radar antenna is faintly visible below the wing and fuselage.

A light-colored AN/APQ-7 radar antenna is slung underneath a B-29B with black camouflage on the undersides. Although the tail is clipped off in this photo, the plane likely was assigned to the 315th Bombardment Wing.

The majority of the B-29Bs were assigned to the 315th Bombardment Wing in the Marianas. This assemblage of B-29Bs wears the B-in-a-diamond tail symbol of the 16th Bombardment Group of the 315th Wing. The second plane in line is nicknamed "Loaded Dice," with accompanying artwork of two dice. *National Archives*

The Museum of Aviation, Robins Air Force Base, Georgia, preserves as a static display Bell-Marietta B-29B-55-BA, serial number 44-84053. The museum recovered this Superfortress from Aberdeen Proving Ground, Maryland, in 1983. The plane was completed in July 1945. Robbins Air Force Base is of significance in the B-29 story, since hundreds of Superfortresses were encased in plastic film and placed in long-term storage there following World War II and then were put back in service for the Korean War. *Author photo*

The Strategic Air Command & Aerospace Museum, Ashland, Nebraska, preserves B-29B-20-BA, serial number 44-84076, which was converted to a TB-29B trainer after delivery to the Army Air Forces. The plane was displayed outdoors at the Strategic Air Command Museum, Bellevue, Nebraska, from 1959 to 1997, when the plane was placed on display indoors at the Strategic Air Command & Aerospace Museum. An extended and thorough restoration of the bomber commenced in 2006. *Author photo*

B-29B Serial Numbers

Production block	Starting serial number	Ending serial number
B-29B-30-BA	42-63581	42-63621
B-29B-35-BA	42-63622	42-63691
B-29B-40-BA	42-63692	42-63736
B-29B-40-BA	42-63738	42-63743
B-29B-40-BA	42-63745	42-63749
B-29B-40-BA	42-63751	
B-29B-40-BA	44-83890	44-83893
B-29B-40-BA	44-83895	
B-29B-45-BA	44-83896	44-83899
B-29B-45-BA	44-83901	44-83903
B-29B-45-BA	44-83905	44-83907
B-29B-45-BA	44-83909	44-83910
B-29B-45-BA	44-83912	44-83913
B-29B-45-BA	44-83915	44-83916
B-29B-45-BA	44-83918	44-83919
B-29B-45-BA	44-83921	44-83922
B-29B-45-BA	44-83924	44-83925
B-29B-45-BA	44-83927	
B-29B-45-BA	44-83929	
B-29B-45-BA	44-83931	
B-29B-45-BA	44-83933	
B-29B-45-BA	44-83935	
B-29B-45-BA	44-83937	
B-29B-45-BA	44-83939	
B-29B-45-BA	44-83941	44-83944
B-29B-45-BA	44-83946	
B-29B-45-BA	44-83948	
B-29B-45-BA	44-83950	
B-29B-45-BA	44-83952	
B-29B-45-BA	44-83954	
B-29B-45-BA	44-83956	
B-29B-45-BA	44-83958	44-83959
B-29B-45-BA	44-83961	
B-29B-50-BA	44-83963	
B-29B-50-BA	44-83965	
B-29B-50-BA	44-83967	

Production block	Starting serial number	Ending serial number
B-29B-50-BA	44-83969	
B-29B-50-BA	44-83971	
B-29B-50-BA	44-83973	
B-29B-50-BA	44-83975	
B-29B-50-BA	44-83977	
B-29B-50-BA	44-83979	
B-29B-50-BA	44-83981	
B-29B-50-BA	44-83983	
B-29B-50-BA	44-83985	
B-29B-50-BA	44-83985	
B-29B-50-BA	44-83987	
B-29B-50-BA	44-83989	
B-29B-50-BA	44-83991	
B-29B-50-BA	44-83993	
B-29B-50-BA	44-83995	
B-29B-50-BA	44-83997	
B-29B-50-BA	44-83999	
B-29B-50-BA	44-84001	
B-29B-50-BA	44-84003	
B-29B-50-BA	44-84005	
B-29B-50-BA	44-84007	
B-29B-55-BA	44-84009	
B-29B-55-BA	44-84011	
B-29B-55-BA	44-84013	
B-29B-55-BA	44-84015	
B-29B-55-BA	44-84017	
B-29B-55-BA	44-84019	
B-29B-55-BA	44-84021	
B-29B-55-BA	44-84023	
B-29B-55-BA	44-84025	
B-29B-55-BA	44-84027	
B-29B-55-BA	44-84029	
B-29B-55-BA	44-84031	
B-29B-55-BA	44-84033	
B-29B-55-BA	44-84035	
B-29B-55-BA	44-84037	
B-29B-55-BA	44-84039	
B-29B-55-BA	44-84041	

Production block	Starting serial number	Ending serial number
B-29B-55-BA	44-84043	
B-29B-55-BA	44-84045	
B-29B-55-BA	44-84047	
B-29B-55-BA	44-84049	
B-29B-55-BA	44-84051	
B-29B-55-BA	44-84053	
B-29B-55-BA	44-84055	
B-29B-60-BA	44-84057	
B-29B-60-BA	44-84059	
B-29B-60-BA	44-84061	
B-29B-60-BA	44-84063	
B-29B-60-BA	44-84065	
B-29B-60-BA	44-84067	
B-29B-60-BA	44-84069	
B-29B-60-BA	44-84071	
B-29B-60-BA	44-84073	
B-29B-60-BA	44-84075	
B-29B-60-BA	44-84077	
B-29B-60-BA	44-84079	
B-29B-60-BA	44-84081	
B-29B-60-BA	44-84083	
B-29B-60-BA	44-84085	
B-29B-60-BA	44-84087	
B-29B-60-BA	44-84089	
B-29B-60-BA	44-84091	
B-29B-60-BA	44-84093	
B-29B-60-BA	44-84095	
B-29B-60-BA	44-84097	
B-29B-60-BA	44-84099	
B-29B-60-BA	44-84101	
B-29B-60-BA	44-84103	
B-29B-65-BA	44-84105	
B-29B-65-BA	44-84107	
B-29B-65-BA	44-84109	
B-29B-65-BA	44-84111	
B-29B-65-BA	44-84113	
B-29B-65-BA	44-84115	
B-29B-65-BA	44-84117	

Production block	Starting serial number	Ending serial number
B-29B-65-BA	44-84119	
B-29B-65-BA	44-84121	
B-29B-65-BA	44-84123	
B-29B-65-BA	44-84125	
B-29B-65-BA	44-84127	
B-29B-65-BA	44-84129	
B-29B-65-BA	44-84131	
B-29B-65-BA	44-84133	
B-29B-65-BA	44-84135	
B-29B-65-BA	44-84137	
B-29B-65-BA	44-84139	
B-29B-65-BA	44-84141	
B-29B-65-BA	44-84143	
B-29B-65-BA	44-84145	
B-29B-65-BA	44-84147	
B-29B-65-BA	44-84149	
B-29B-65-BA	44-84151	
B-29B-65-BA	44-84155	

CHAPTER 7

The Photo Birds: F-13/F-13A

The long-range and high-altitude capabilities of the B-29 made it a logical candidate for use as a photoreconnaissance aircraft. Although this work was authorized in May 1944, it would be August 4, 1944, before the first of the modified aircraft flew. That aircraft, B-29-20-BW, serial number 42-6412, through the installation of a variety of camera gear, became the first F-13 Superfortress.

Subsequently, a further forty factory-new B-29s were converted to F-13 configuration, as were ninety-seven B-29As, which became F-13A aircraft. All of these conversions were performed at the Denver Modification Center. The aircraft were typically equipped with a trimetrogon camera arrangement consisting of three K-17B 6-inch cameras and two 40-inch K-22 cameras. The aircraft carried the normal eleven-man B-29 crew, plus a photographer and camera man.

To fulfill a 1943 USAAF requirement for a long-range, high-altitude photoreconnaissance aircraft, a total of 138 B-29-BWs and B-29As were equipped with mounts and windows for cameras and were designated, respectively, F-13 and F-13A. Various complements of camera models were possible; a typical installation included three K-17B, one K-18, and two K-22 cameras. The cameras were mounted in the unpressurized part of the aft fuselage. Bomb-bay fuel tanks frequently were installed, to extend the range. Shown here is an F-13 converted from B-29-40-BW, serial number 42-24583. While serving with the 497th Bombardment Group, this plane was ditched on account of engine failure off Agana, Guam, on June 8, 1945.

In a left-rear view of Boeing-Wichita F-13-40-BW, serial number 42-24583, the camera ports are lost in the shadows on the lower part of the fuselage. The turrets were retained on the F-13s and F-13As.

Camera windows on the left side of the fuselage of F-13A-50-BN, serial number 44-61822, are depicted. These windows comprised ¾-inch flat-glass plates. A window for a side-pointing camera is aft of the national insignia, and four additional windows for oblique windows are toward the bottom of the fuselage.

Camera windows on the right side of F-13A, serial number 44-61822, are documented in an August 1946 photograph. To the upper left is the aft crew door.

The flat-glass windows for cameras on the belly of F-13A, serial number 44-61822, are viewed facing forward. Note the radome on the belly between the bomb bays.

An April 24, 1947, photograph shows modifications to the camera well in the aft unpressurized compartment of an F-13, facing forward. Note the seat to the upper left.

Vertical cameras installed in F-13A, serial number 44-61822, are viewed facing aft in an August 1946 photograph.

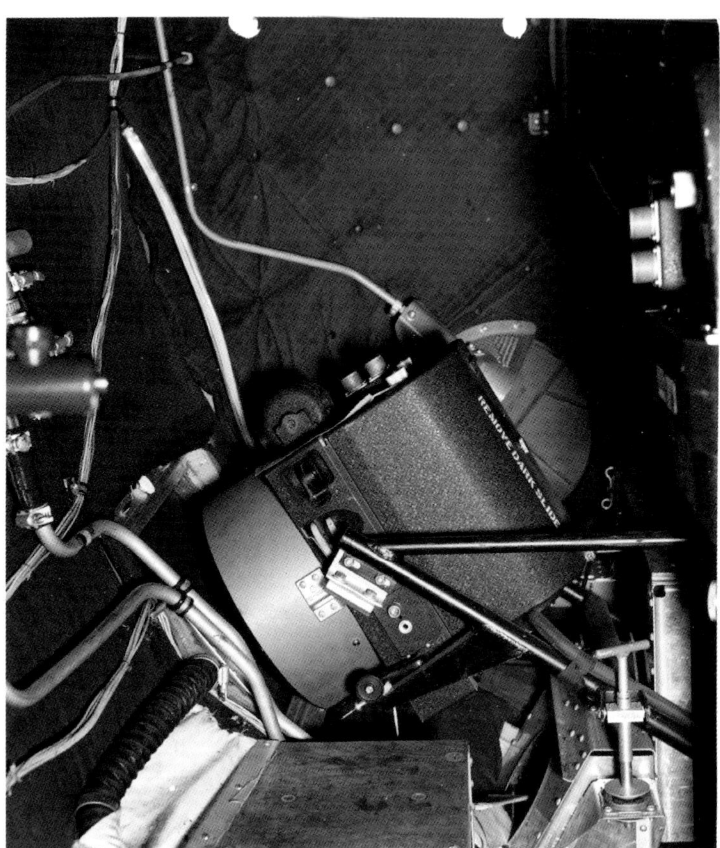

In the same F-13A, an oblique camera installation on the right side of the fuselage is viewed facing aft.

The camera sighting for the F-13/F-13A was in the bombardier's compartment, and a modified-drift sight (normally used for calculating the plane's deviation from its intended course) was used for sighting the cameras, as seen at the lower center of this photo inside F-13A, serial number 44-61822. To the left is the right side of a Norden bombsight.

A final photo of F-13A, serial number 44-61822, depicts the navigator's compartment just aft of the cockpit on the left side, facing aft and to the left, with the navigator's seat to the lower left and his desk in the lower foreground.

CHAPTER 8

The Experimentals: XB-39/XB-44

XB-39

As described earlier in this volume, the B-29 (as well as the B-32) program was initially plagued with problems with the Wright R-3350-12 engine. As a result, the Army Air Force sought an alternative power plant. The alternative engine was the Allison V-3420 liquid-cooled engine. Somewhat ironically, development of this engine, which was essentially two V-1710 engines mated to a common crankcase, had begun in 1937 but had been plagued with problems of its own.

When the concept of repowering the B-29 with the V-3420 began, B-29s were in critically short supply. Thus, the decision was made to use the Douglas XB-19, then the world's largest bomber, as a test bed for the project, a fitting choice since the XB-19 had actually been designed to use the V-3420, but delays in development of that engine had forced it to be fitted with radials instead.

The conversion of the XB-19 to V-3420 power was accomplished by the Fisher Body Cleveland Aircraft plant, a facility originally constructed to produce B-29 bombers. The XB-19A, as the modified aircraft was designated, was completed in late July 1944. When testing revealed the combination was successful, including increased performance, the decision was made to proceed with the installation of the Allisons on a Superfortress. The first YB-29, serial number 41-36954, nicknamed "Spirit of Lincoln," was flown to Cleveland for conversion to XB-39 configuration, powered by four V-3420 engines.

In September 1944, the Army Air Forces requested forty-five additional modifications to the base aircraft, including replacement of the entire fuel system. Implementing these changes not surprisingly delayed the conversion work. But in mid-November the XB-39 was ready for flight testing. Ground tests in the Cleveland winter revealed that the turbosuperchargers were freezing. As a temporary expedient, the turbos were bypassed, and the XB-39 took to the air for the first time on December 9, 1944.

While the XB-39 performed satisfactorily, by this time great strides had been made in solving the R-3350 problems, while diagnosing the issues with the V-3420 had just begun. Hence, the XB-39 project was abandoned.

XB-44

Even after production of the B-29 was well underway, it was apparent that the R-3350 Duplex Cyclone engines were operating at their limits. In an effort to increase power, the decision was made to attempt the installation of the Pratt & Whitney R-4360 Wasp Major engines—the largest piston aircraft engine ever mass-produced in the US.

B-29A-5-BN, serial number 42-93845, was provided to Pratt & Whitney for this purpose. Pratt & Whitney replaced the four R-3350s, 2,200 horsepower each, with a quartet of their 3,000-horsepower Wasp Major engines.

When flight testing of the XB-44 began in May 1944, the new aircraft proved to be 50–60 mph faster than the B-29. In July 1945, 200 production examples were ordered, which were to be designated B-29D.

The end of the war brought about the cancellation of the B-29D contract before any were produced. However, the concept of an R-4360-powered Superfortress was far from dead and would resurface almost immediately in the post–World War II era.

Because of the tendency of the Wright R-3550 engines in the early B-29s to fail or catch fire, experiments were conducted with the Allison V-3420 water-cooled engine as a replacement. General Motors converted the first YB-29, serial number 41-36954, "Spirit Of Lincoln," by installing four V-3420 power plants, along with new engine nacelles and propeller spinners. In this configuration, the aircraft was redesignated the XB-39.

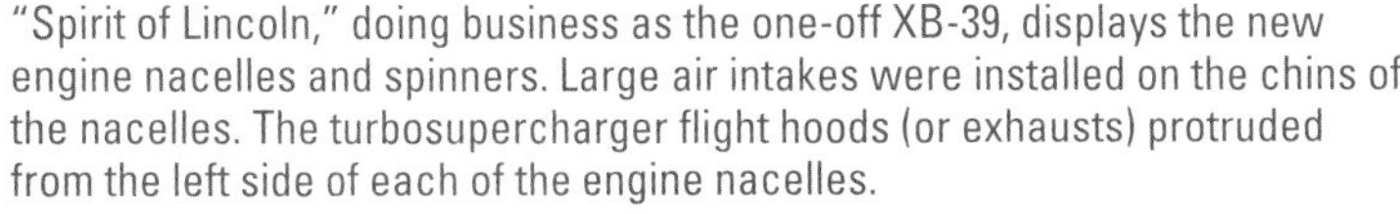
"Spirit of Lincoln," doing business as the one-off XB-39, displays the new engine nacelles and spinners. Large air intakes were installed on the chins of the nacelles. The turbosupercharger flight hoods (or exhausts) protruded from the left side of each of the engine nacelles.

Both of the Allison V-3420 engines in the XB-39 basically were two Allison V-1710 V-12 liquid-cooled engines that drove a single propeller shaft. The XB-39 prototype failed to result in a production model.

Because the B-29's Wright R-3350 engines were considered somewhat underpowered for the weight of the aircraft, experiments were conducted with an installation of more-powerful Pratt & Whitney Wasp Major twenty-eight-cylinder, 3,000-horsepower engines in a B-29A, serial number 42-93845. As seen in this photo of the one-off prototype aircraft, designated the XB-44, the engine nacelles featured a large air scoop on the bottom for the oil coolers and intercoolers.

The XB-44 first flew in May 1945. This in-flight view of the XB-44 shows further details of the engine nacelles and cowlings. The successful testing of the XB-44 would lead to an order for a production version, the B-29D, which would be redesignated the B-50 in late 1945.